ric little bandbox of a ballpark.

s in curiously sharp focus, like

ng-type Easter egg. It was

offers, as do most Boston

s Euclidean ᵈᵃᵗᵃᵏᵐᵢᵐᵃˣⁱᵐ

g irregularities. Right field is

erican league, ʷʰᵃⁿˣ while left

ft field wall, 315 feet ˣᵐˣᵍ

ᵗʰˣᵐᵏˢ from home plate along,

its surface at right-handed

dnesday, September 28th, as I

formed groundskeeper was

picking batting-practice home-rums

athere℄ seen in Wordsworthian

d uninspirational; the Red Sox

Also by John Updike

HUB FANS BID KID ADIEU

Hub Fans Bid Kid Adieu

John Updike *on* Ted Williams

A Special Publication of
The Library of America

Copyright © 2010 by The Estate of John Updike
Copyright 1965, 1991, 2007 by John Updike

Published by arrangement with Alfred A. Knopf,
an imprint of The Knopf Doubleday Publishing Group,
a division of Random House, Inc.

Frontispiece: Ted Williams ascends to the Fenway field,
September 28, 1960. Photograph by Dick Thompson,
courtesy The Sports Museum, Boston.

Endpapers: From the setting copy of "Hub Fans Bid Kid Adieu,"
mailed by the author to *The New Yorker* on October 5, 1960.
Courtesy Houghton Library, Harvard University,
by permission of The Estate of John Updike.

Case: The Kid knocks another one out of Fenway Park: a moment
from the mid-1940s. Photograph by Leslie Jones, courtesy
The Boston Public Library Print Department.

Distributed to the trade by Penguin Group USA Inc.
and in Canada by Penguin Group Canada Ltd.

Design by David Bullen Design

Library of Congress Control Number 2009934632
ISBN 978-1-59853-071-1

Manufactured in the United States of America
First printing

ACKNOWLEDGMENTS

"Hub Fans Bid Kid Adieu" first appeared in *The New Yorker*, October 20, 1960, and was reprinted, with added footnotes, in *Assorted Prose* (1965). Parts of "Ted Williams, 1918–2002" first appeared in two essays, one in *Sport*, December 1986, the other in *The New York Times Magazine*, December 29, 2002; later versions were printed, respectively, in *Odd Jobs* (1991) and *Due Considerations* (2007).

CONTENTS

PREFACE

"Hub Fans Bid Kid Adieu" was a five days' labor of love executed and published in October 1960. For many years, especially since moving to Greater Boston, I had been drawing sustenance and cheer from Williams' presence on the horizon, and I went to his last game with the open heart of a fan. The events there compelled me to become a reporter. As I hurriedly composed this account, the facts were all in me, ready to be plucked, fifteen years' accumulation. When I included the piece in a 1965 collection, *Assorted Prose*, I added, as footnotes, some additional information not then available to me. They stand as of 1965.

At the time of its magazine acceptance, the editor of *The New Yorker*, William Shawn, told me, graciously, that it was the best piece about baseball they had ever printed. This was a smaller compliment than it seems, for among Harold Ross's many prejudices was one against baseball, and the magazine up to 1960 had contained few words on the subject. Thurber's excellent baseball tall tale, "You Could Look It Up," had been published elsewhere. Since the sixties, of course, Roger Angell has covered the beat more than amply; inexhaustibly enraptured by the action on the field, omnisciently informed about our overexpanded leagues, Angell is a baseball freak where I was just a Williams freak. But I like to think I made *The New Yorker* safe for the Great American Game.

The piece was admired. The late George Frazier, who often put my name in his *Boston Globe* compilations of people who lacked *Duende*, identified it as the only decent thing I'd ever written. The compliment that meant most to me came from Williams himself, who through an agent invited me to write his biography. I declined the honor. I had said all I had to say, for that matter about every professional sport except golf. I did, however, write a mid-life sketch of Williams for *Sport* Magazine in 1986, and an obituary for *The New York Times Magazine* in 2002. They are abridged, conflated, and updated here under the heading "Ted Williams, 1918–2002."

Romances sneak up on us. Once, at the age of twelve, on the awninged side porch of a pal's house in Shillington, Pa., I found myself holding a board-game card marked "Williams."

Each card in the set had a punched-out center, around which was a circle divided proportionately to the named batter's percentages (singles, doubles, walks, etc.). To play the game, as I remember, you fitted the card onto a spinner, flicked the arrow, and advanced a token base runner accordingly. My *Schlag-ballbewußtsein* (see footnote, page 5) had not yet dawned; I had heard of DiMaggio, but not of Williams. Yet this strange bland name, not to be confused with Esther, was better; his arc of hits was immense. And he was mine. That day began the romance, the internalized ups and downs, whose last act was my attending a cloudy-day contest in late September, 1960, in Fenway Park.

J. U.

January 2009

HUB FANS BID KID ADIEU

Fenway Park, in Boston, is a lyric little bandbox of a ballpark. Everything is painted green and seems in curiously sharp focus, like the inside of an old-fashioned peeping-type Easter egg. It was built in 1912 and rebuilt in 1934, and offers, as do most Boston artifacts, a compromise between Man's Euclidean determinations and Nature's beguiling irregularities. Its right field is one of the deepest in the American League, while its left field is the shortest; the high left-field wall, three hundred and fifteen feet from home plate along the foul line, virtually thrusts its surface at right-handed hitters. On the afternoon of Wednesday, September 28th, 1960, as I took a seat behind third base, a uniformed groundkeeper was treading the top of this wall, picking batting-practice home runs out of the screen, like a mushroom gatherer seen in Wordsworthian perspective on the verge of a cliff. The day was overcast, chill, and uninspirational. The Boston team was the worst in twenty-seven seasons. A jangling medley of incompetent youth and aging competence, the Red Sox were finishing in seventh place only because the Kansas City Athletics had locked them out of the cellar. They were scheduled to play the Baltimore Orioles, a much nimbler blend of May and December, who had been dumped from pennant contention a week before by the insatiable Yankees. I, and 10,453 others, had shown up primarily because this was the Red Sox' last home game of the season, and therefore the last time in all eternity that their regular left fielder, known to the headlines as TED, KID, SPLINTER, THUMPER, TW, and, most cloyingly, MISTER WONDERFUL, would play in Boston. "WHAT WILL WE DO WITHOUT TED? HUB FANS ASK" ran the headline on a newspaper being read by a bulb-nosed cigar smoker a few rows away. Williams' retirement had been announced, doubted (he had been threatening retirement for years), confirmed by Tom Yawkey, the Red Sox owner, and at last widely accepted as the sad but probable truth. He was forty-two and had redeemed his abysmal season of 1959 with a—considering his advanced age—fine one. He had been giving away his gloves and bats and had grudgingly consented to a sentimental ceremony today. This was not necessarily his last game; the Red Sox were scheduled to travel to New York and wind up the season with three games there.

I arrived early. The Orioles were hitting fungos on the field. The day before, they had spitefully smothered the Red Sox, 17–4, and neither their faces nor their drab gray visiting-team uniforms seemed very gracious. I wondered who had invited them to the party. Between our heads and the lowering clouds a frenzied organ was thundering through, with an appositeness perhaps accidental, "You *maaaade* me love you, I didn't wanna do it, I didn't wanna do it. . . ."

❖

The affair between Boston and Ted Williams was no mere summer romance; it was a marriage, composed of spats, mutual disappointments, and, toward the end, a mellowing hoard of shared memories. It fell into three stages, which may be termed Youth, Maturity, and Age; or Thesis, Antithesis, and Synthesis; or Jason, Achilles, and Nestor.

First, there was the by now legendary epoch[1] when the

1. This piece was written with no research materials save an outdated record book and the Boston newspapers of the day; and Williams' early career preceded the dawning of my *Schlagballbewußtsein* (Baseball-consciousness). Also for reasons of perspective was my account of his beginnings skimped.

young bridegroom came out of the West and announced "All I want out of life is that when I walk down the street folks will say 'There goes the greatest hitter who ever lived.'" The dowagers of local journalism attempted to give elementary deportment

---

Williams first attracted the notice of a major-league scout—Bill Essick of the Yankees—when he was a fifteen-year-old pitcher with the San Diego American Legion Post team. As a pitcher-outfielder for San Diego's Herbert Hoover High School, Williams recorded averages of .586 and .403. Essick balked at signing Williams for the $1,000 his mother asked; he was signed instead, for $150 a month, by the local Pacific Coast League franchise, the newly created San Diego Padres. In his two seasons with this team, Williams hit merely .271 and .291, but his style and slugging (23 home runs the second year) caught the eye of, among others, Casey Stengel, then with the Boston Braves, and Eddie Collins, the Red Sox general manager. Collins bought him from the Padres for $25,000 in cash and $25,000 in players. Williams was then nineteen. Collins' fond confidence in the boy's potential matched Williams' own. Williams reported to the Red Sox training camp in Sarasota in 1938 and, after showing more volubility than skill, was shipped down to the Minneapolis Millers, the top Sox farm team. It should be said, perhaps, that the parent club was equipped with an excellent, if mature, outfield, mostly purchased from Connie Mack's dismantled A's. Upon leaving Sarasota, Williams is supposed to have told the regular outfield of Joe Vosmik, Doc Cramer, and Ben Chapman that he would be back and would make more money than the three of them put together. At Minneapolis he hit .366, batted in 142 runs, scored 130, and hit 43 home runs. He also loafed in the field, jabbered at the fans, and smashed a water cooler with his fist. In 1939 he came north with the Red Sox. On the

lessons to this child who spake as a god, and to their horror
were themselves rebuked. Thus began the long exchange of
backbiting, bat-flipping, booing, and spitting that has distin-
guished Williams' public relations.[2] The spitting incidents of

---

way, in Atlanta, he dropped a foul fly, accidentally kicked it away in trying
to pick it up, picked it up, and threw it out of the park. It would be nice if,
his first time up in Fenway Park, he had hit a home run. Actually, in his first
Massachusetts appearance, the first inning of an exhibition game against Holy
Cross at Worcester, he *did* hit a home run, a grand slam. The Red Sox season
opened in Yankee Stadium. Facing Red Ruffing, Williams struck out and,
the next time up, doubled for his first major-league hit. In the Fenway Park
opener, against Philadelphia, he had a single in five trips. His first home run
came on April 23, in that same series with the A's. Williams was then twenty,
and played *right* field. In his rookie season, he hit .327; in 1940, .344.

  2. See *Ted Williams*, by Ed Linn (Sport Magazine Library, 1961), Chapter
6, "Williams vs. the Press." It is Linn's suggestion that Williams walked into
a circulation war among the seven Boston newspapers, who in their com-
petitive zeal headlined incidents that the New York papers, say, would have
minimized, just as they minimized the less genial side of the moody and aloof
DiMaggio and smoothed Babe Ruth into a folk hero. It is also Linn's thought,
and an interesting one, that Williams thrived on even adverse publicity and
needed a hostile press to elicit, contrariwise, his defiant best. The statistics
(especially of the 1958 season, when he snapped a slump by spitting in all
directions, and inadvertently conked an elderly female fan with a tossed bat)
seem to corroborate this. Certainly Williams could have had a truce for the
asking, and his industrious perpetuation of the war, down to his last day in

1957 and 1958 and the similar dockside courtesies that Williams has now and then extended to the grandstand should be judged against this background: the left-field stands at Fenway for twenty years have held a large number of customers who have bought their way in primarily for the privilege of showering abuse on Williams. Greatness necessarily attracts debunkers, but in Williams' case the hostility has been systematic and unappeasable. His basic offense against the fans has been to wish that they weren't there. Seeking a perfectionist's vacuum, he has quixotically desired to sever the game from the ground of paid spectatorship and publicity that supports it. Hence his refusal to tip his cap[3] to the crowd or turn the other cheek to

---

uniform, implies its usefulness to him. The actual and intimate anatomy of the matter resides in locker rooms and hotel corridors fading from memory. When my admiring account was printed, I received a letter from a sports reporter who hated Williams with a bitter and explicit immediacy. And even Linn's hagiology permits some glimpses of Williams' locker-room manners that are not pleasant.

3. But he did tip his cap, high off his head, in at least his first season, as cartoons from that period verify. He was also extravagantly cordial to taxi drivers and stray children. See Linn, Chapter 4, "The Kid Comes to Boston": "There has never been a ballplayer—anywhere, anytime—more popular than Ted Williams in his first season in Boston." To this epoch belongs Williams'

newsmen. It has been a costly theory—it has probably cost him, among other evidences of good will, two Most Valuable Player awards, which are voted by reporters[4]—but he has held to it. While his critics, oral and literary, remained beyond the reach of his discipline, the opposing pitchers were accessible, and he spanked them to the tune of .406 in 1941.[5] He slumped to .356 in 1942 and went off to war.

In 1946, Williams returned from three years as a Marine

---

prankish use of the Fenway scoreboard lights for rifle practice, his celebrated expressed preference for the life of a fireman, and his determined designation of himself as "The Kid."

4. In 1947 Joe DiMaggio and in 1957 Mickey Mantle, with seasons inferior to Williams', won the MVP award because sportswriters, who vote on ballots with ten places, had vengefully placed Williams ninth, tenth, or nowhere at all. The 1941 award to Joe DiMaggio, even though this was Williams' .406 year, is more understandable, since this was also the *annus miraculorum* when DiMaggio hit safely in fifty-six consecutive games.

5. The sweet saga of this beautiful decimal must be sung once more. Williams, after hitting above .400 all season, had cooled to .39955 with one doubleheader left to play, in Philadelphia. Joe Cronin, then managing the Red Sox, offered to bench him to safeguard his average, which was exactly .400 when rounded to the third decimal place. Williams said (I forget where I read this) that he did not want to become the .400 hitter with just his toenails over the line. He played the first game and singled, homered, singled, and

pilot to the second of his baseball avatars, that of Achilles,
the hero of incomparable prowess and beauty who nevertheless was to be found sulking in his tent while the Trojans
(mostly Yankees) fought through to the ships. Yawkey, a tim-
ber and mining maharajah, had surrounded his central jewel
with many gems of slightly lesser water, such as Bobby Doerr,
Dom DiMaggio, Rudy York, Birdie Tebbetts, and Johnny
Pesky. Throughout the late forties, the Red Sox were the best
paper team in baseball, yet they had little three-dimensional
to show for it, and if this was a tragedy, Williams was Ham-
let. A succinct review of the indictment—and a fair sample
of appreciative sports-page prose—appeared the very day of
Williams' valedictory, in a column by Huck Finnegan in the
Boston American (no sentimentalist, Huck):

> *Williams' career, in contrast [to Babe Ruth's], has been a*
> *series of failures except for his averages. He flopped in the*

---

singled. With less to gain than to lose, he elected to play the second game and
got two more hits, including a double that dented a loudspeaker horn on the
top of the right-field wall, giving him six for eight on the day and a season's
average that, in the forty years between Rogers Hornsby's .403 (1925) and the
present, stands as unique.

only World Series he ever played in (1946) when he batted only .200. He flopped in the playoff game with Cleveland in 1948. He flopped in the final game of the 1949 season with the pennant hinging on the outcome (Yanks 5, Sox 3). He flopped in 1950 when he returned to the lineup after a two-month absence and ruined the morale of a club that seemed pennant-bound under Steve O'Neill. It has always been Williams' records first, the team second, and the Sox non-winning record is proof enough of that.

There are answers to all this, of course. The fatal weakness of the great Sox slugging teams was not-quite-good-enough pitching rather than Williams' failure to hit a home run every time he came to bat. Again, Williams' depressing effect on his teammates has never been proved. Despite ample coaching to the contrary, most insisted that they *liked* him. He was generous with advice to any player who asked for it. In an increasingly combative baseball atmosphere, he continued to duck beanballs docilely. With umpires he was gracious to a fault. This courtesy itself annoyed his critics, whom there was no pleasing. And against the ten crucial games (the seven World Series games with the St. Louis Cardinals, the 1948 playoff with the Cleveland Indians, and the two-game series with the Yankees at the end of the 1949 season, winning either one of which would have given the Red Sox the pennant) that make up the Achilles' heel of Williams' record, a mass of statistics can be set showing that day in and day out he was no slouch in the clutch.[6] The correspondence columns of the Boston papers now and then suffer a sharp flurry of arithmetic on this score; indeed, for Williams to have distributed all his hits so they did nobody else any good would constitute a feat of placement unparalleled in the annals of selfishness.

◆

Whatever residue of truth remains of the Finnegan charge those of us who love Williams must transmute as best we can, in our own personal crucibles. My personal memories of Williams began when I was a boy in Pennsylvania, with two last-place teams in Philadelphia to keep me company. For

---

6. For example: In 1948, the Sox came from behind to tie the Indians by winning three straight; in those games Williams went two for two, two for two, and two for four. In 1949, the Sox overtook the Yankees by winning nine in a row; in that streak, Williams won four games with home runs.

me, "W'ms, lf" was a figment of the box scores who always seemed to be going three for five. He radiated, from afar, the hard blue glow of high purpose. I remember listening over the radio to the All-Star Game of 1946, in which Williams hit two singles and two home runs, the second one off a Rip Sewell "blooper" pitch; it was like hitting a balloon out of the park. I remember watching one of his home runs from the bleachers of Shibe Park; it went over the first baseman's head and rose methodically along a straight line and was still rising when it cleared the fence. The trajectory seemed qualitatively different from anything anyone else might hit. For me, Williams is the classic ballplayer of the game on a hot August weekday, before a small crowd, when the only thing at stake is the tissue-thin difference between a thing done well and a thing done ill. Baseball is a game of the long season, of relentless and gradual averaging-out. Irrelevance—since the reference point of most individual contests is remote and statistical—always threatens its interest, which can be maintained not by the occasional heroics that sportswriters feed upon but by players who always *care*; who care, that is to say, about themselves and their art. Insofar as the clutch hitter is not a sportswriter's myth, he is a vulgarity, like a writer who writes only for money. It may be that, compared to such managers' dreams as the manifestly classy Joe DiMaggio and the always-helpful Stan Musial, Williams was an icy star. But of all team sports, baseball, with its graceful intermittences of action, its immense and tranquil field sparsely settled with poised men in white, its dispassionate mathematics, seems to me best suited to accommodate, and be ornamented by, a loner. It is an essentially lonely game. No other player visible to my generation concentrated within himself so much of the sport's poignance, so assiduously refined his natural skills, so constantly brought to the plate that intensity of competence that crowds the throat with joy.

By the time I went to college, near Boston, the lesser stars Yawkey had assembled around Williams had faded, and his rigorous pride of craftsmanship had become itself a kind of heroism. This brittle and temperamental player developed an unexpected quality of persistence. He was always coming back—back from Korea, back from a broken collarbone, a shattered elbow, a bruised heel, back from drastic bouts of flu and ptomaine poisoning. Hardly a season went by without some enfeebling mishap, yet he always came back, and always looked like himself. The delicate mechanism of timing and power seemed sealed, shockproof, in some place deep within his frame.[7] In addition to injuries, there was a heavily publicized divorce, and the usual storms with the press, and the Williams Shift—the maneuver, custom-built by Lou Boudreau of the Cleveland Indians, whereby three infielders were concentrated on the right side of the infield.[8] Williams could easily have learned to punch singles through the vacancy on his left

---

7. Two reasons for his durability may be adduced. A non-smoker, nondrinker, habitual walker, and year-round outdoorsman, Williams spared his body the vicissitudes of the seasonal athlete. And his hitting was in large part a mental process; the amount of cerebration he devoted to such details as pitchers' patterns, prevailing winds, and the muscular mechanics of swinging a bat would seem ridiculous if it had not paid off. His intellectuality, as it were, perhaps explains the quickness with which he adjusted, after the war, to the changed conditions—the night games, the addition of the slider to the standard pitching repertoire, the new cry for the long ball. His reaction to the Williams Shift, then, cannot be dismissed as unconsidered.

8. Invented, or perpetrated (as a joke?), by Boudreau on July 14, 1946, between games of a doubleheader. In the first game of the doubleheader, Williams had hit three homers and batted in eight runs. The shift was not used when men were on base and, had Williams bunted or hit late against it immediately, it might not have spread, in all its variations, throughout the league. The

and fattened his average hugely. This was what Ty Cobb, the Einstein of average, told him to do. But the game had changed since Cobb; Williams believed that his value to the club and to the league was as a slugger, so he went on pulling the ball, trying to blast it through three men, and paid the price of perhaps fifteen points of lifetime average. Like Ruth before him, he bought the occasional home run at the cost of many directed singles—a calculated sacrifice certainly not, in the case of a hitter as average-minded as Williams, entirely selfish.

After a prime so harassed and hobbled, Williams was granted by the relenting fates a golden twilight. He became at the end of his career perhaps the best *old* hitter of the century. The dividing line falls between the 1956 and the 1957 seasons. In September of the first year, he and Mickey Mantle were contending for the batting championship. Both were hitting around .350, and there was no one else near them. The season ended with a three-game series between the Yankees and the Sox, and, living in New York then, I went up to the Stadium.

Cardinals used it in the lamented World Series of that year. Toward the end, in 1959 and 1960, rather sadly, it had faded from use, or degenerated to the mere clockwise twitching of the infield customary against pull hitters.

Williams was slightly shy of the four hundred at-bats needed to qualify; the fear was expressed that the Yankee pitchers would walk him to protect Mantle. Instead, they pitched to him. It was wise. He looked terrible at the plate, tired and discouraged and unconvincing. He never looked very good to me in the Stadium.[9] The final outcome in 1956 was Mantle .353, Williams .345.

The next year, I moved from New York to New England, and it made all the difference. For in September of 1957, in the same situation, the story was reversed. Mantle finally hit .365; it was the best season of his career. But Williams, though sick and old, had run away from him. A bout of flu had laid him low in September. He emerged from his cave in the Hotel Somerset haggard but irresistible; he hit four successive pinch-hit home runs. "I feel terrible," he confessed, "but every time I take a swing at the ball it goes out of the park." He ended the

---

9. Shortly before his retirement, Williams, in *Life*, wrote gloomily of the Stadium, "There's the bigness of it. There are those high stands and all those people smoking—and, of course, the shadows. . . . It takes at least one series to get accustomed to the Stadium and even then you're not sure." Yet his lifetime batting average there is .340, only four points under his median average.

season with thirty-eight home runs and an average of .388, the highest in either league since his own .406, and, coming from a decrepit man of thirty-nine, an even more supernal figure. With eight or so of the "leg hits" that a younger man would have beaten out, it would have been .400. And the next year, Williams, who in 1949 and 1953 had lost batting championships by decimal whiskers to George Kell and Mickey Vernon, sneaked in behind his teammate Pete Runnels and filched his sixth title, a bargain at .328.

In 1959, it seemed all over. The dinosaur thrashed around in the .200 swamp for the first half of the season, and was even benched ("rested," Manager Mike Higgins tactfully said). Old foes like the late Bill Cunningham began to offer batting tips. Cunningham thought Williams was jiggling his elbows;[10] in

---

10. It was Cunningham who, when Williams first appeared in a Red Sox uniform at the 1938 spring training camp, wrote with melodious prescience: "The Sox seem to think Williams is just cocky enough and gabby enough to make a great and colorful outfielder, possibly the Babe Herman type. Me? I don't like the way he stands at the plate. He bends his front knee inward and moves his foot just before he takes a swing. That's exactly what I do before I drive a golf ball, and knowing what happens to the golf balls I drive, I don't believe this kid will ever hit half a Singer Midget's weight in a bathing suit."

truth, Williams' neck was so stiff he could hardly turn his head to look at the pitcher. When he swung, it looked like a Calder mobile with one thread cut; it reminded you that since 1954 Williams' shoulders had been wired together. A solicitous pall settled over the sports pages. In the two decades since Williams had come to Boston, his status had imperceptibly shifted from that of a naughty prodigy to that of a municipal monument. As his shadow in the record books lengthened, the Red Sox teams around him declined, and the entire American League seemed to be losing life and color to the National. The inconsistency of the new superstars—Mantle, Colavito, and Kaline—served to make Williams appear all the more singular. And off the field, his private philanthropy—in particular, his zealous chairmanship of the Jimmy Fund, a charity for children with cancer—gave him a civic presence matched only by that of Richard Cardinal Cushing. In religion, Williams appears to be a humanist, and a selective one at that, but he and the abrasive-voiced cardinal, when their good works intersect and they appear in the public eye together, make a handsome pair of seraphim.

Humiliated by his '59 season, Williams determined, once

more, to come back. I, as a specimen Williams partisan, was both glad and fearful. All baseball fans believe in miracles; the question is, how *many* do you believe in? He looked like a ghost in spring training. Manager Billy Jurges warned us ahead of time that if Williams didn't come through he would be benched, just like anybody else. As it turned out, it was Jurges who was benched. Williams entered the 1960 season needing eight home runs to have a lifetime total of 500; after one time at bat, in Washington, he needed seven. For a stretch, he was hitting a home run every second game that he played. He passed Lou Gehrig's lifetime total, and finished with 521, thirteen behind Jimmie Foxx, who alone stands between Williams and Babe Ruth's unapproachable 714. The summer was a statistician's picnic. His two-thousandth walk came and went, his eighteen-hundredth run batted in, his sixteenth All-Star Game. At one point, he hit a home run off a pitcher, Don Lee, off whose father, Thornton Lee, he had hit a home run a generation before. The only comparable season for a forty-two-year-old man was Ty Cobb's in 1928. Cobb batted .323 and hit one homer. Williams batted .316 but hit twenty-nine homers.

In sum, though generally conceded to be the greatest hitter of his era, he did not establish himself as "the greatest hitter who ever lived." Cobb, for average, and Ruth, for power, remain supreme. Cobb, Rogers Hornsby, Joe Jackson, and Lefty O'Doul, among players since 1900, have higher lifetime averages than Williams' .344. Unlike Foxx, Gehrig, Hack Wilson, Hank Greenberg, and Ralph Kiner, Williams never came close to matching Babe Ruth's season home-run total of sixty.[11] In the list of major-league batting records, not one is held by Williams. He is second in walks drawn, third in home runs, fifth in lifetime average, sixth in runs batted in, eighth in runs scored and in total bases, fourteenth in doubles, and thirtieth in hits. But if we allow him merely average seasons for the four-plus seasons he lost to two wars, and add another season for the months he lost to injuries, we get a man who in all the power totals would be second, and not a very distant second, to Ruth. And if we further allow that these years would have been not merely average but prime years, if we allow for all

---

11. Written in 1960, a year before Roger Maris's fluky, phenomenal sixty-one.

the months when Williams was playing in sub-par condition, if we permit his early and later years in baseball to be some sort of index of what the middle years could have been, if we give him a right-field fence that is not, like Fenway's, one of the most distant in the league, and if—the least excusable "if"—we imagine him condescending to outsmart the Williams Shift, we can defensibly assemble, like a colossus induced from the sizable fragments that do remain, a statistical figure not incommensurate with his grandiose ambition. From the statistics that are on the books, a good case can be made that in the *combination* of power and average Williams is first; nobody else ranks so high in both categories. Finally, there is the witness of the eyes; men whose memories go back to Shoeless Joe Jackson—another unlucky natural—rank him and Williams together as the best-looking hitters they have seen. It was for our last look that ten thousand of us had come.

◆

Two girls, one of them with pert buckteeth and eyes as black as vest buttons, the other with white skin and flesh-colored hair, like an underdeveloped photograph of a redhead, came and sat on my right. On my other side was one of those frowning chestless young-old men who can frequently be seen, often wearing sailor hats, attending ball games alone. He did not once open his program but instead tapped it, rolled up, on his knee as he gave the game his disconsolate attention. A young lady, with freckles and a depressed, dainty nose that by an optical illusion seemed to thrust her lips forward for a kiss, sauntered down into the box seat right behind the roof of the Orioles dugout. She wore a blue coat with a Northeastern University emblem sewed to it. The girls beside me took it into their heads that this was Williams' daughter. She looked too old to me, and why would she be sitting behind the visitors' dugout? On the other hand, from the way she sat there, staring at the sky and French-inhaling, she clearly was *somebody*. Other fans came and eclipsed her from view. The crowd looked less like a weekday ballpark crowd than like the folks you might find in Yellowstone National Park, or emerging from automobiles at the top of scenic Mount Mansfield. There were a lot of competitively well-dressed couples of tourist age, and not a few babes in arms. A row of five seats in front of me was abruptly filled with a woman and four children, the youngest of them two years old, if that. Someday, presumably, he could tell his grandchildren that he saw Williams play. Along with these tots and second-honeymooners, there were Harvard freshmen, giving off that peculiar nervous glow created when a sufficient quantity of insouciance is saturated with enough insecurity; thick-necked Army officers with brass on their shoulders and steel in their stares; pepperings of priests; perfumed bouquets of Roxbury Fabian fans; shiny salesmen from Albany and Fall River; and those gray, hoarse men—taxi drivers, slaughterers, and bartenders—who will continue to click through the turnstiles long after everyone else has deserted to television and tramporamas. Behind me, two young male voices blossomed, cracking a joke about God's five proofs that Thomas Aquinas exists—typical Boston College levity.

The batting cage was trundled away. The Orioles fluttered to the sidelines. Diagonally across the field, by the Red Sox dugout, a cluster of men in overcoats were festering like maggots. I could see a splinter of white uniform, and Williams' head, held at a self-deprecating and evasive tilt. Williams' conversational stance is that of a six-foot-three-inch man under a six-foot ceiling. He moved away to the patter of flash bulbs, and began playing catch with a young Negro outfielder named Willie Tasby. His arm, never very powerful, had grown lax with the years, and his throwing motion was a kind of muscular drawl. To catch the ball, he flicked his glove hand onto his left shoulder (he batted left but threw right, as every schoolboy ought to know) and let the ball plop into it comically. This catch session with Tasby was the only time all afternoon I saw him grin.

A tight little flock of human sparrows who, from the lambent and pampered pink of their faces, could only have been Boston politicians moved toward the plate. The loudspeakers mammothly coughed as someone huffed on the microphone. The ceremonies began. Curt Gowdy, the Red Sox radio and television announcer, who sounds like everybody's brother-in-law, delivered a brief sermon, taking the two words "pride" and "champion" as his text. It began, "Twenty-one years ago, a skinny kid from San Diego, California . . ." and ended, "I don't think we'll ever see another like him." Robert Tibolt, chairman of the board of the Greater Boston Chamber of Commerce, presented Williams with a big Paul Revere silver bowl. Harry

Carlson, a member of the sports committee of the Boston Chamber, gave him a plaque, whose inscription he did not read in its entirety, out of deference to Williams' distaste for this sort of fuss. Mayor Collins, seated in a wheelchair, presented the Jimmy Fund with a thousand-dollar check.

Then the occasion himself stooped to the microphone, and his voice sounded, after the others, very Californian; it seemed to be coming, excellently amplified, from a great distance, adolescently young and as smooth as a butternut. His thanks for the gifts had not died from our ears before he glided, as if helplessly, into "In spite of all the terrible things that have been said about me by the knights of the keyboard up there . . ." He glanced up at the press rows suspended above home plate. The crowd tittered, appalled. A frightful vision flashed upon me, of the press gallery pelting Williams with erasers, of Williams clambering up the foul screen to slug journalists, of a riot, of Mayor Collins being crushed. ". . . And they *were* terrible things," Williams insisted, with level melancholy, into the mike. "I'd like to forget them, but I can't." He paused, swallowed his memories, and went on, "I want to say that my years in Boston have been the greatest thing in my life." The crowd, like an immense sail going limp in a change of wind, sighed with relief. Taking all the parts himself, Williams then acted out a vivacious little morality drama in which an imaginary tempter came to him at the beginning of his career and said, "Ted, you can play anywhere you like." Leaping nimbly into the role of his younger self (who in biographical actuality had yearned to be a Yankee), Williams gallantly chose Boston over all the other cities, and told us that Tom Yawkey was the greatest owner in baseball and we were the greatest fans. We applauded ourselves heartily. The umpire came out and dusted the plate. The voice of doom announced over the loudspeakers that after Williams' retirement his uniform number, 9, would be permanently retired—the first time the Red Sox had so honored a player. We cheered. The national anthem was played. We cheered. The game began.

❖

Williams was third in the batting order, so he came up in the bottom of the first inning, and Steve Barber, a young pitcher born two months before Williams began playing in the major leagues, offered him four pitches, at all of which he disdained to swing, since none of them were within the strike zone. This demonstrated simultaneously that Williams' eyes were razor-sharp and that Barber's control wasn't. Shortly, the bases were full, with Williams on second. "Oh, I hope he gets held up at third! That would be wonderful," the girl beside me moaned, and, sure enough, the man at bat walked and Williams was delivered into our foreground. He struck the pose of Donatello's David, the third-base bag being Goliath's head. Fiddling with his cap, swapping small talk with the Orioles third baseman (who seemed delighted to have him drop in), swinging his arms with a sort of prancing nervousness, he looked fine—flexible, hard, and not unbecomingly substantial through the middle. The long neck, the small head, the knickers whose cuffs were worn down near his ankles—all these clichés of sports-cartoon iconography were rendered in the flesh.

With each pitch, Williams danced down the baseline, waving his arms and stirring dust, ponderous but menacing, like an attacking goose. It occurred to about a dozen humorists at once to shout "Steal home! Go, go!" Williams' speed afoot was never legendary. Lou Clinton, a young Sox outfielder, hit a fairly deep fly to center field. Williams tagged up and ran home. As he slid across the plate, the ball, thrown with unusual heft by Jackie Brandt, the Orioles center fielder, hit him on the back.

"Boy, he was really loafing, wasn't he?" one of the collegiate voices behind me said.

"It's cold," the other explained. "He doesn't play well when it's cold. He likes heat. He's a hedonist."

The run that Williams scored was the second and last of the inning. Gus Triandos, of the Orioles, quickly evened the score by plunking a home run over the handy left-field wall. Williams, who had had this wall at his back for twenty years,[12] played the ball flawlessly. He didn't budge. He just stood there, in the center of the little patch of grass that his patient footsteps had worn brown, and, limp with lack of interest, watched the ball pass overhead. It was not a very interesting game. Mike Higgins, the Red Sox manager, with nothing to lose, had restricted his major-league players to the left-field line—along with Williams, Frank Malzone, a first-rate third

---

12. In his second season (1940) he was switched to left field, to protect his eyes from the right-field sun.

baseman, played the game—and had peopled the rest of the terrain with unpredictable youngsters fresh, or not so fresh, off the farms. Other than Williams' recurrent appearances at the plate, the *maladresse* of the Sox infield was the sole focus of suspense; the second baseman turned every grounder into a juggling act, while the shortstop did a breathtaking impersonation of an open window. With this sort of assistance, the Orioles wheedled their way into a 4–2 lead. They had early replaced Barber with another young pitcher, Jack Fisher. Fortunately (as it turned out), Fisher is no cutie; he is willing to burn the ball through the strike zone, and inning after inning this tactic punctured Higgins' string of test balloons.

Whenever Williams appeared at the plate—pounding the dirt from his cleats, gouging a pit in the batter's box with his left foot, wringing resin out of the bat handle with his vehement grip, switching the stick at the pitcher with an electric ferocity—it was like having a familiar Leonardo appear in a shuffle of *Saturday Evening Post* covers. This man, you realized—and here, perhaps, was the difference, greater than the difference in gifts—really desired to hit the ball. In the third inning, he hoisted a high fly to deep center. In the fifth, we thought he had it; he smacked the ball hard and high into the heart of his power zone, but the deep right field in Fenway and the heavy air and a casual east wind defeated him. The ball died. Al Pilarcik leaned his back against the big "380" painted on the right-field wall and caught it. On another day, in another park, it would have been gone. (After the game, Williams said, "I didn't think I could hit one any harder than that. The conditions weren't good.")

The afternoon grew so glowering that in the sixth inning the arc lights were turned on—always a wan sight in the daytime, like the burning headlights of a funeral procession. Aided by the gloom, Fisher was slicing through the Sox rookies, and Williams did not come to bat in the seventh. He was second up in the eighth. This was almost certainly his last time to come to the plate in Fenway Park, and instead of merely cheering, as we had at his three previous appearances, we stood, all of us, and applauded. I had never before heard pure applause in a ballpark. No calling, no whistling, just an ocean of handclaps, minute after minute, burst after burst, crowding and running together in continuous succession like the pushes of surf at the edge of the sand. It was a somber and considered tumult. There was not a boo in it. It seemed to renew itself out of a shifting set of memories as the Kid, the Marine, the veteran of feuds and failures and injuries, the friend of children, and the enduring old pro evolved down the bright tunnel of twenty-two summers toward this moment. At last, the umpire signaled for Fisher to pitch; with the other players, he had been frozen in position. Only Williams had moved during the ovation, switching his bat impatiently, ignoring everything except his cherished task. Fisher wound up, and the applause sank into a hush.

Understand that we were a crowd of rational people. We knew that a home run cannot be produced at will; the right pitch must be perfectly met and luck must ride with the ball. Three innings before, we had seen a brave effort fail. The air was soggy, the season was exhausted. Nevertheless, there will always lurk, around the corner in a pocket of our knowledge of the odds, an indefensible hope, and this was one of the times, which you now and then find in sports, when a density of expectation hangs in the air and plucks an event out of the future.

Fisher, after his unsettling wait, was low with the first pitch.

He put the second one over, and Williams swung mightily and missed. The crowd grunted, seeing that classic swing, so long and smooth and quick, exposed. Fisher threw the third time, Williams swung again, and there it was. The ball climbed on a diagonal line into the vast volume of air over center field. From my angle, behind third base, the ball seemed less an object in flight than the tip of a towering, motionless construct, like the Eiffel Tower or the Tappan Zee Bridge. It was in the books while it was still in the sky. Brandt ran back to the deepest corner of the outfield grass, the ball descended beyond his reach and struck in the crotch where the bullpen met the wall, bounced chunkily, and vanished.

Like a feather caught in a vortex, Williams ran around the square of bases at the center of our beseeching screaming. He ran as he always ran out home runs—hurriedly, unsmiling, head down, as if our praise were a storm of rain to get out of. He didn't tip his cap. Though we thumped, wept, and chanted "We want Ted" for minutes after he hid in the dugout, he did not come back. Our noise for some seconds passed beyond excitement into a kind of immense open anguish, a wailing, a cry to be saved. But immortality is nontransferable. The papers said that the other players, and even the umpires on the field, begged him to come out and acknowledge us in some way, but he refused. Gods do not answer letters.

◆

Every true story has an anticlimax. The men on the field refused to disappear, as would have seemed decent, in the smoke of Williams' miracle. Fisher continued to pitch, and escaped further harm. At the end of the inning, Higgins sent Williams out to his left-field position, then instantly replaced him with Carroll Hardy, so we had a long last look at Williams as he ran out there and then back, his uniform jogging, his eyes steadfast on the ground. It was nice, and we were grateful, but it left a funny taste.

One of the scholasticists behind me said, "Let's go. We've seen everything. I don't want to spoil it." This seemed a sound aesthetic decision. Williams' last word had been so exquisitely chosen, such a perfect fusion of expectation, intention, and execution, that already it felt a little unreal in my head, and I wanted to get out before the castle collapsed. But the game, though played by clumsy midgets under the feeble glow of the arc lights, began to tug at my attention, and I loitered in the runway until it was over. Williams' homer had, quite incidentally, made the score 4–3. In the bottom of the ninth inning, with one out, Marlan Coughtry, the second-base juggler, singled. Vic Wertz, pinch-hitting, doubled off the left-field wall, Coughtry advancing to third. Pumpsie Green walked, to load the bases. Willie Tasby hit a double-play ball to the third baseman, but in making the pivot throw Billy Klaus, an ex–Red Sox infielder, reverted to form and threw the ball past the first baseman and into the Red Sox dugout. The Sox won, 5–4. On the car radio as I drove home I heard that Williams, his own man to the end, had decided not to accompany the team to New York. He had met the little death that awaits athletes. He had quit.

TED WILLIAMS, 1918–2002

ＴED TOOK HIS TIME leaving this world, and he's not quite out of it yet. He is cryonically frozen in Arizona, drained of blood and upside down but pretty much intact,[1] waiting for whatever resurrection technology can eventually produce. This bizarre turn in the Williams saga, which two of his three children claim to be by his own wish, does accord with a general perception among his admirers that there was something very precious about him, worth preserving if at all possible. To those of us who saw him at the plate, he seemed the concentrated essence of baseball: a tall, long-necked man wringing the bat handle and snapping the slender implement of Kentucky ash back and forth, back and forth in his impatience to hit the ball, to win the battle of wits and eye-hand coordination that, inning after inning, pits the solitary batter against the nine opposing men on the field.

---

1. It's worse than I thought: his head has been severed and is preserved. His body? Who knows? The engineer of the remains' disposal, Williams' only son, the unfortunate John Henry, himself died in 2004, of leukemia, at the age of thirty-five.

He came from California to a dowdy New England metropolis with too many newspapers, and was instant news. The Williams excitement had to do with his personality as well as his prowess; the former was as complex as the latter seemed transparent. He was, like Ty Cobb, a deprived man, hungry for greatness; but, unlike Cobb, he had a sweet smile. Boston wanted to love the Kid, but he was prickly in its embrace. He was hot-tempered and rabbit-eared and became contemptuous of sportswriters and too proud to tip his hat after hitting a home run. And the teams he ornamented didn't win all the marbles; the spectacular Sox of 1946 lost the World Series, and, after that, pennants just slipped away, while Williams sulked, spat, threw bats, and threatened retirement. In the end, the city loved him all the more because the relationship had proved so complex; "some obstacle," as Freud wrote, "is necessary to swell the tide of libido to its height." No sports hero—not Bobby Orr or Larry Bird or Rocky Marciano— had a greater hold over the fans of New England than Ted Williams.

He had talent: a big man with great eyes. He had intensity, and nobody practiced longer or thought harder about the niceties of the little war between pitchers and hitters. But he also had poignance, a flair for the dramatic. His career abounds with storybook hits, with thunder that remained etched on the air. But behind all that thunder stood a multitude of hot days and wearisome nights, games that didn't mean much beyond the moment, to which Williams brought his electric, elegant best. We loved him because he generated excitement: he lifted us out of our lives and showed us, in the way he stood up at the plate, what the game was all about.

For most of two decades—1939 to 1960, with time out for service in two wars—he was the main reason that people went to Red Sox games in Boston.[2] In those decades he made the American League All-Star team eighteen times and had the highest overall batting average, .344. The decades since his retirement, crowded with careers uninterrupted by national service and bolstered by a livelier ball and new techniques of physical conditioning, have seen him slip lower in the record lists; his home-run total of 521, third behind Babe Ruth and

---

2. In 1957 the third-place Sox drew 1,187,087, and the sportswriter Harold Kaese wrote, "The Red Sox drew 187,087 and Ted Williams drew the other million."

Jimmie Foxx in 1960, is now tied for eighteenth, with Frank
Thomas and Willie McCovey. His lifetime on-base percent-
age of .482 still stands as the major-league record, although
the phenomenal Barry Bonds twice had better single seasons
(.609 in 2004, .582 in 2002) than Williams' best (.551 in 1941).
And in the four years from 2001 to 2004, Bonds three times
exceeded a total in which Williams for decades had ranked
only second to Ruth, that of walks drawn in a single season.

One Williams statistic, however, gathers luster rather than
dust as the years go by—his season average, in 1941, of .406.
For nearly seventy years he has remained the last of the .400
hitters, his .406 nailed down in a doubleheader in Philadelphia
that he could have sat out; he was batting .39955, which rounds
up to .400, but he elected to play and went six for eight in the
two games. In fact, he hit .400 in three seasons, counting the
truncated bits of 1952 and '53, when he was drafted into the
Korean War: four hits in ten appearances before he reported
for duty, and thirty-seven in ninety-one when he came back
the following year. In 1957, he hit .388, including four home
runs in as many official at-bats when a bout of flu had reduced
him to a pinch-hitter. That year, and then the next, he became

the oldest man ever to win a batting title—a distinction he held until 2004, when Barry Bonds hit .362 at age forty. In the two preceding seasons, 1954 and '55, Williams had the highest average in the league, but injuries and illness kept him from getting four hundred at-bats. These latter seasons, when he was playing for indifferent teams with an accumulated, under-publicized burden of aches and pains, cemented his claim to be called the greatest hitter of his era, an era that included Joe DiMaggio and Stan Musial.

◆

Yet, when an athlete or opera singer or exhilarating personal-ity dies, it is the live performance we remember, the undu-plicable presence, the shimmer and sparkle perceived from however far back a seat in the audience. Williams' swing was a grand motion, never a lunge or a hasty fending, with a graceful follow-through that left his body yearning toward first base. It was long, much longer than Ruth's (how *did* Ruth hit all those home runs out of that chop?), and beautiful the way Sam Snead's swing was beautiful, all body parts working together and the ball just an incident in the course of the arc. *Pop the hips* was his theory, just like a golf pro's; but the golf ball isn't coming at you at ninety miles an hour with english on it, out of a mess of billboards. There was something very pure and uncontrived about the way he hit. He said he swung slightly upwards, to compensate for the pitcher being raised above the batter; but it didn't look that way. His swing looked level. It took up a lot of space and seemed fully serious in its sweep.

At six foot three, Williams was one of the taller men on the field, and we in the crowd brought with us an awareness, like the layer of cigarette smoke that used to hover under the lights, of his dangerous rage to excel—of his on-field temper tantrums, his spats with the press, his struggles with marriage, and his failure, as the years ground on, to make it back to a World Series and redeem his weak performance in 1946. Success and failure in baseball are right out there for all to see; so is focus on the assigned task. Williams' body language declared that he wanted to be the best, that this was more than a game or a livelihood for him. He was paid, toward the end of his career, a record (believe it or not) $125,000 a season, and after his worst season—his only sub-.300 season, in 1959—he asked management for a pay cut.

In the long stretch after 1946, as the excellent Sox teams of the forties yielded to the mediocre fifties teams, Ted kept up the show. The intensity, the handsome lankiness, the electric hum as the lineup worked around to his turn at bat were summer constants. Fenway Park, in those days, was not always full; the advance-ticket crowds from Maine and New Hampshire hadn't yet materialized in that thinner era, which took its baseball as a homely staple, without luxury boxes. On an impulse, I bought in for a few dollars to his final game, and the park was two-thirds empty. I was moved to write about the events of that game, in part because his departure, taking with it the heart of Boston baseball, had been so meagerly witnessed.

❖

With retirement, slowly, he became what William Butler Yeats called a "smiling public man." The stern, temperamental baseball perfectionist dropped his concentrated air of work-in-progress and joined us on the sidelines. He managed a team, the Washington Senators, with a middle-aged patience. He faithfully showed up at Red Sox spring training and was generous—

in a voice bellicosely loud because flying jets in Korea had
half-deafened him—with advice and praise, to friend and foe
alike. He pursued sport fishing with the same obsessive pas-
sion with which he had analyzed the geometry of the strike
zone. He continued to serve as the symbol of the Jimmy Fund,
which he had animated with a thousand personal encourage-
ments of cancer-stricken children. He used his Baseball Hall
of Fame acceptance speech to plead for the admission of the
great players of the old Negro leagues; in a bygone era when
the majors brimmed with unreconstructed rednecks, he had
welcomed baseball's integration and befriended the Red Sox'
belated black recruits.

He drew closer to his three children, and the public grew
closer to him. The new journalism generated interviews in
which his language, long held to the locker room, was revealed
as bumptiously obscene and youthfully enthusiastic. Compared now with DiMaggio, he appeared more open, less wary,
with nothing to hide and everything to share, as the darkness
of failing eyesight, the helplessness of strokes and daily dialysis,
and the desperate operations that the wealthy and famous
must endure closed in. On two occasions his aging body was

hauled to Boston and he made a show of tipping his cap to the crowd; but we didn't need that. The crowd and Ted always shared what was important, a belief that this boys' game terrifically mattered.

A NOTE ABOUT THE AUTHOR

John Updike was born in 1932, in Shillington, Pennsylvania. He graduated from Harvard College in 1954, and spent a year in Oxford, England, at the Ruskin School of Drawing and Fine Art. From 1955 to 1957 he was a member of the staff of *The New Yorker*, and after 1957 lived in Greater Boston, never more than an hour's drive from Fenway Park. He was the author of more than sixty books, including novels and collections of short stories, poems, and criticism. His fiction won the Pulitzer Prize, the National Book Award, the American Book Award, the National Book Critics Circle Award, the PEN/Faulkner Award, and the Howells Medal, among other honors. His only other book of sportswriting is *Golf Dreams*. John Updike died in January 2009.

and execution, that already it f

I wanted to get out before the c

though played by clumsy midgets

the arc lights, began to plead f

the runway until it was over. W

made the score 4-3. M In the bo

out, Marlin Coughtry, the s

Vic Wertz, pinch-hitting, double

advancing to third. Pum

Willie Tasby hit a double-play b

in making the pivot throw, Billy

reverted to form and threw the b

into the Red Sox dugout. The R

as I drove home I heard that Wil

team to New York. So he knew ho

thing. Quit.